CREATURE FEATURE

COLORING

DESIGNED BY

TOM & JAMIE ASCHENBACH

ILLUSTRATED BY TOM ASCHENBACH

I0481467

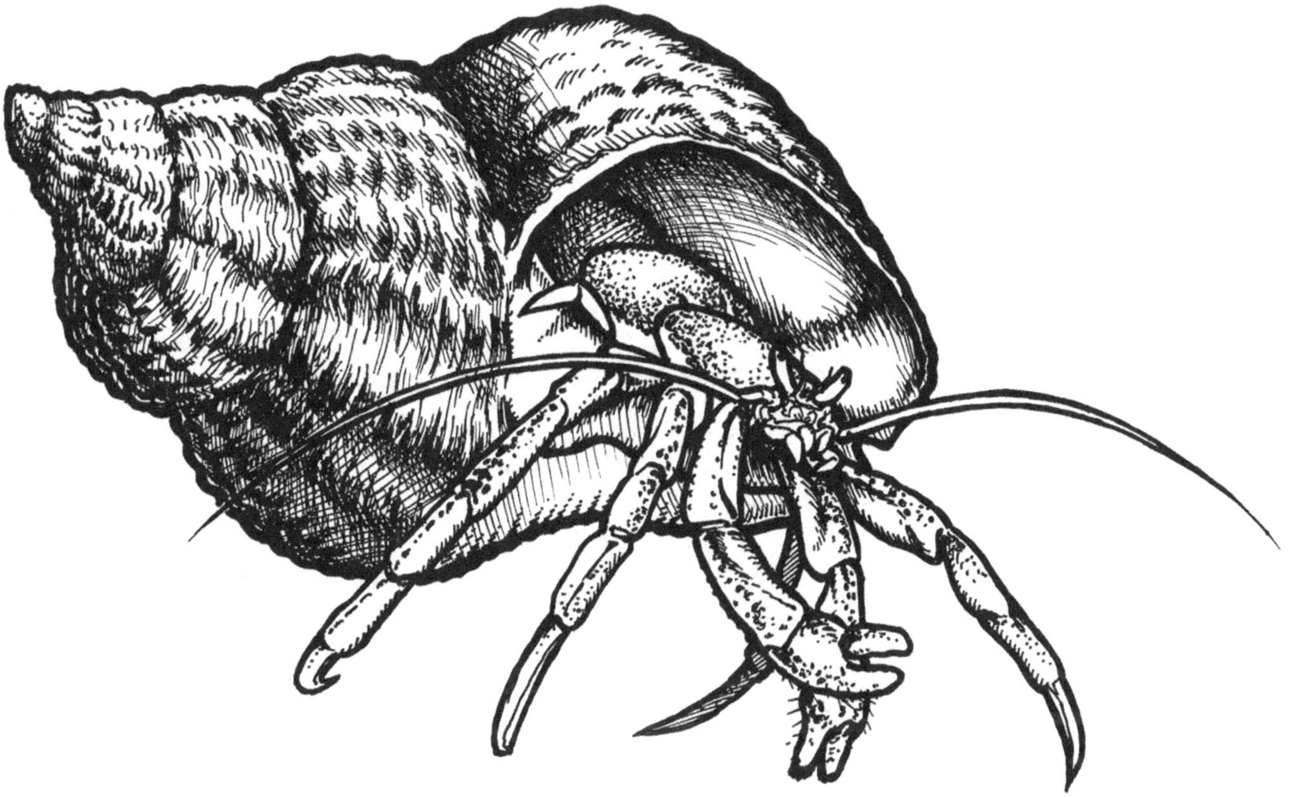

www.facebook.com/TomAschenbachArtist/

ISBN: 1983934585

ISBN-13: 978-1983934582

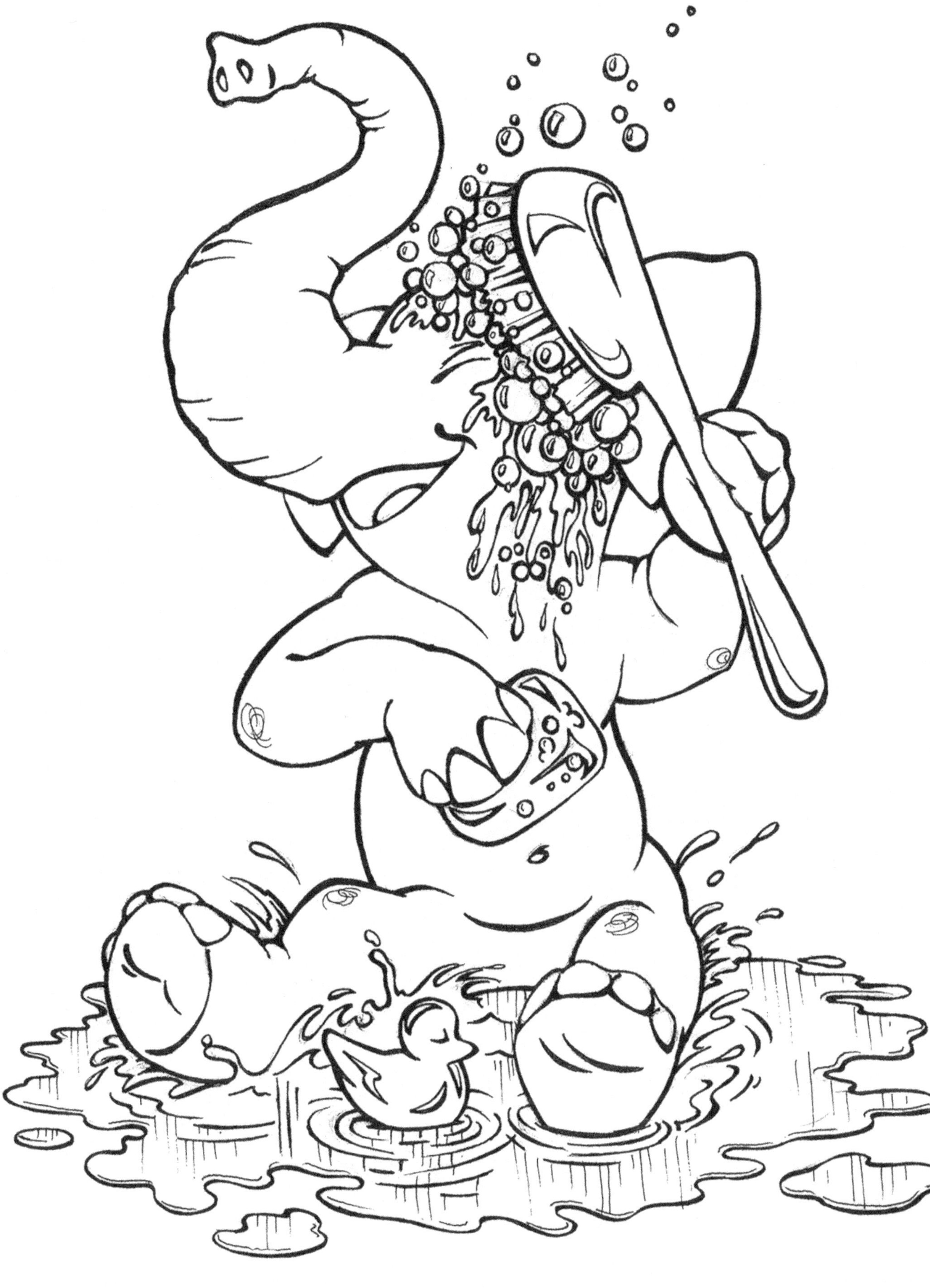

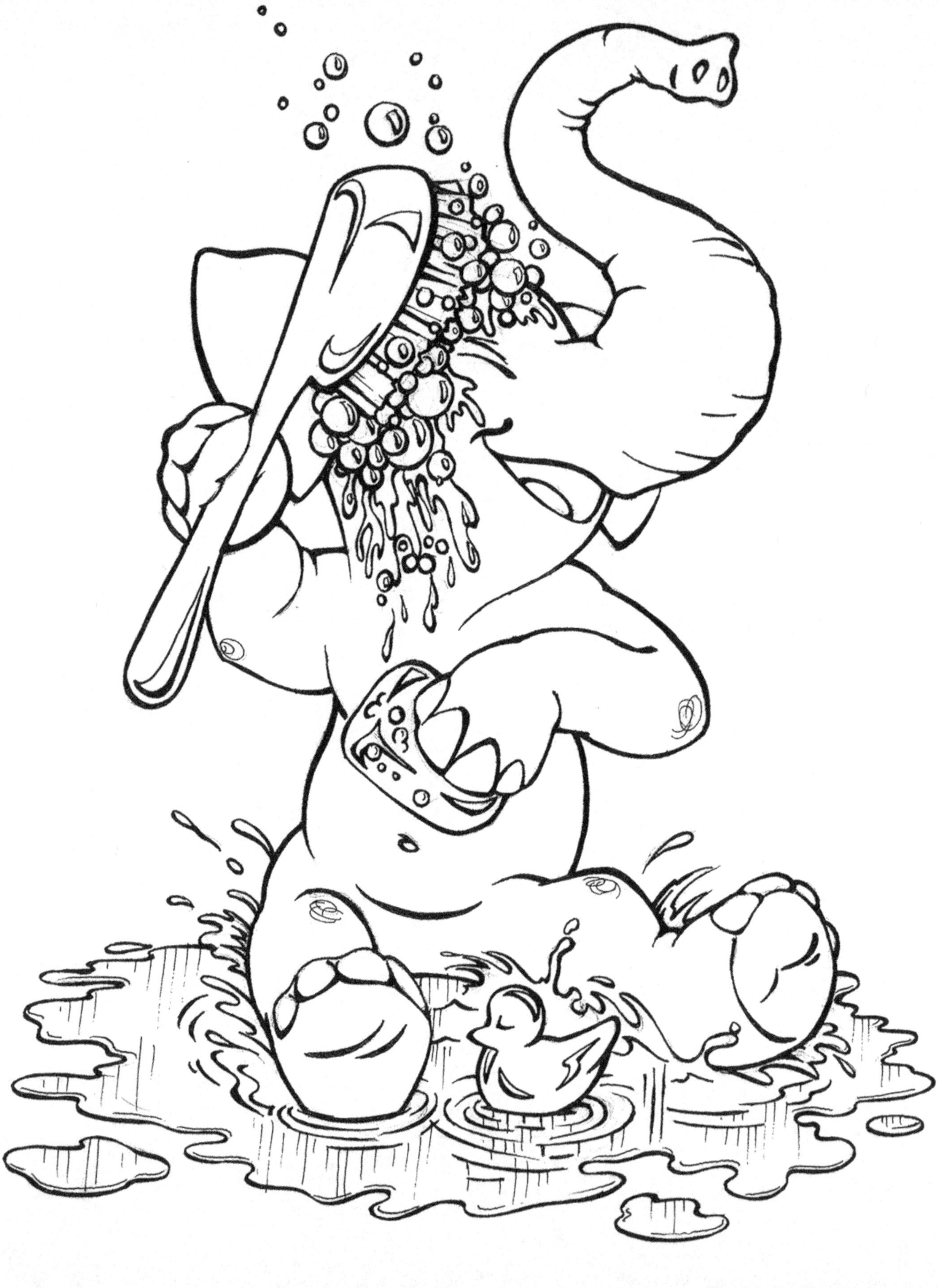

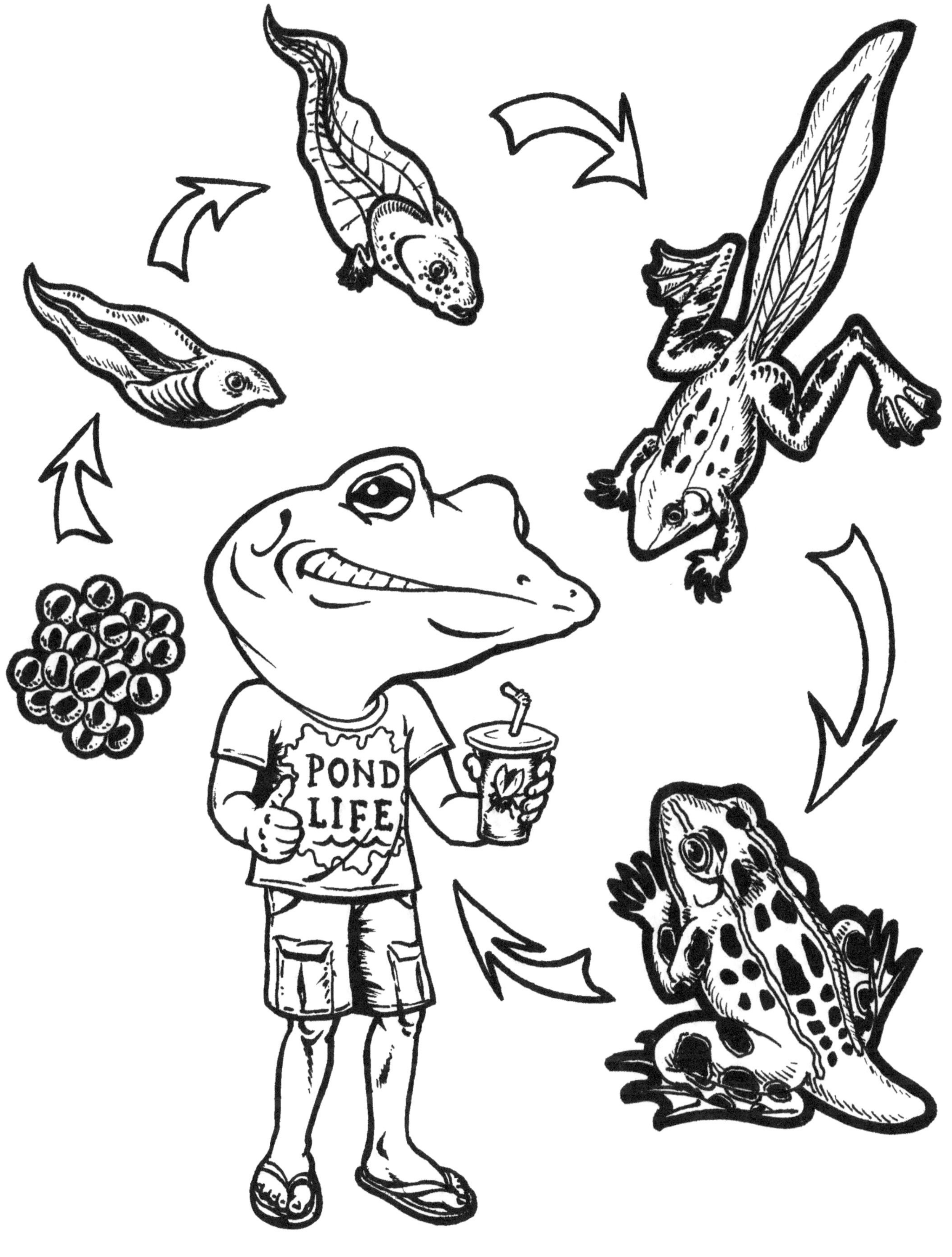
POND
LIFE

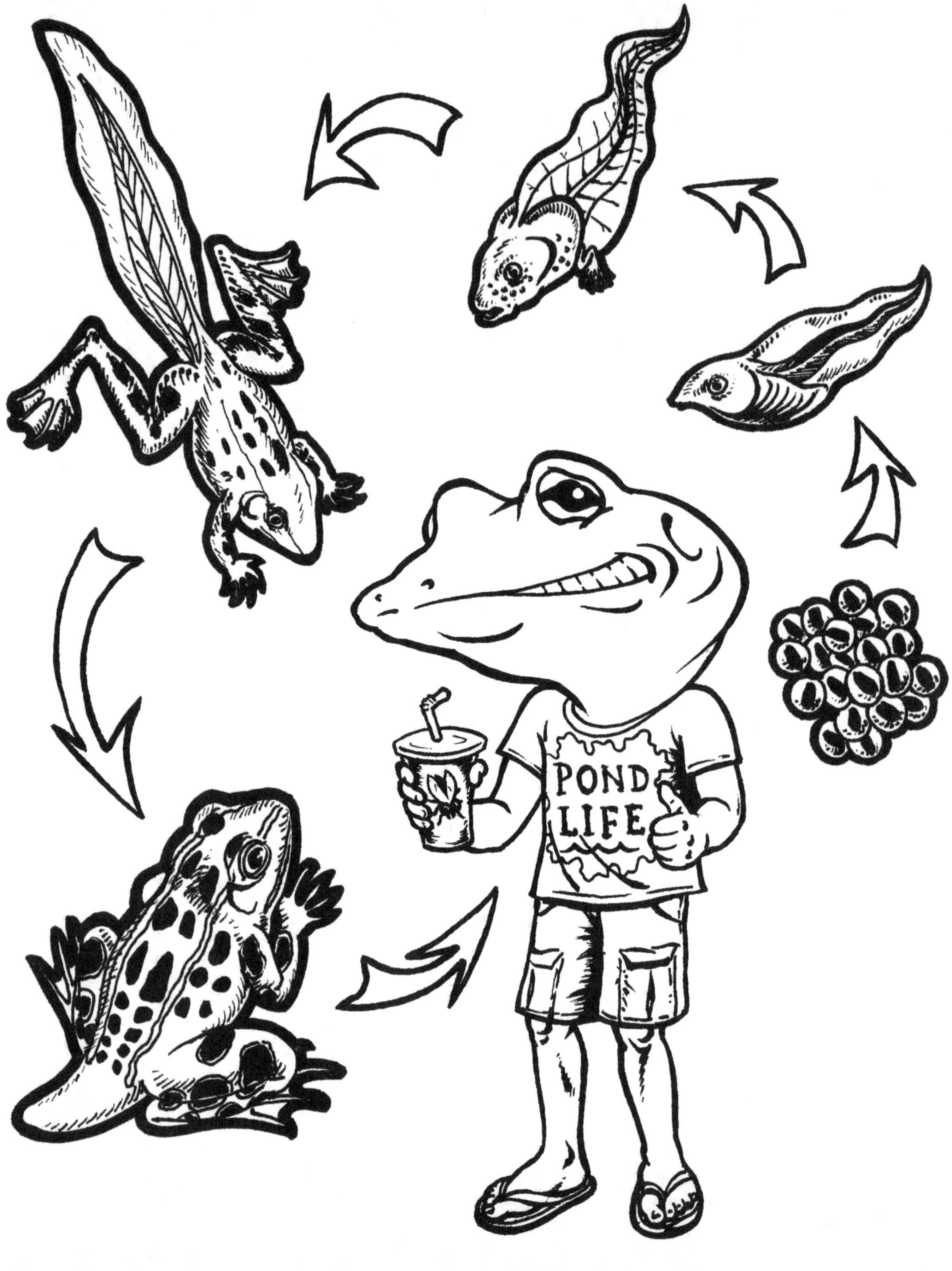
POND
LIFE

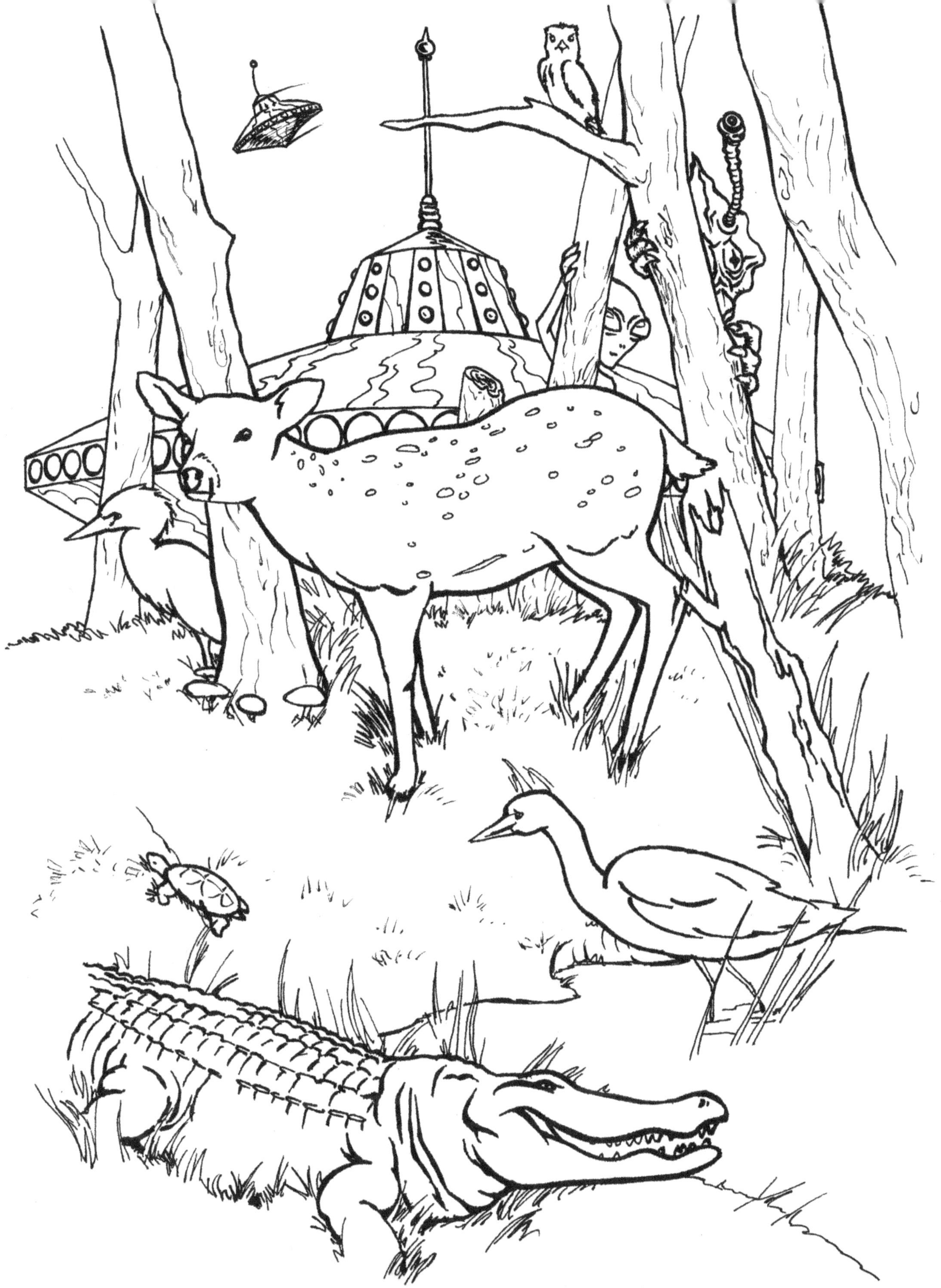

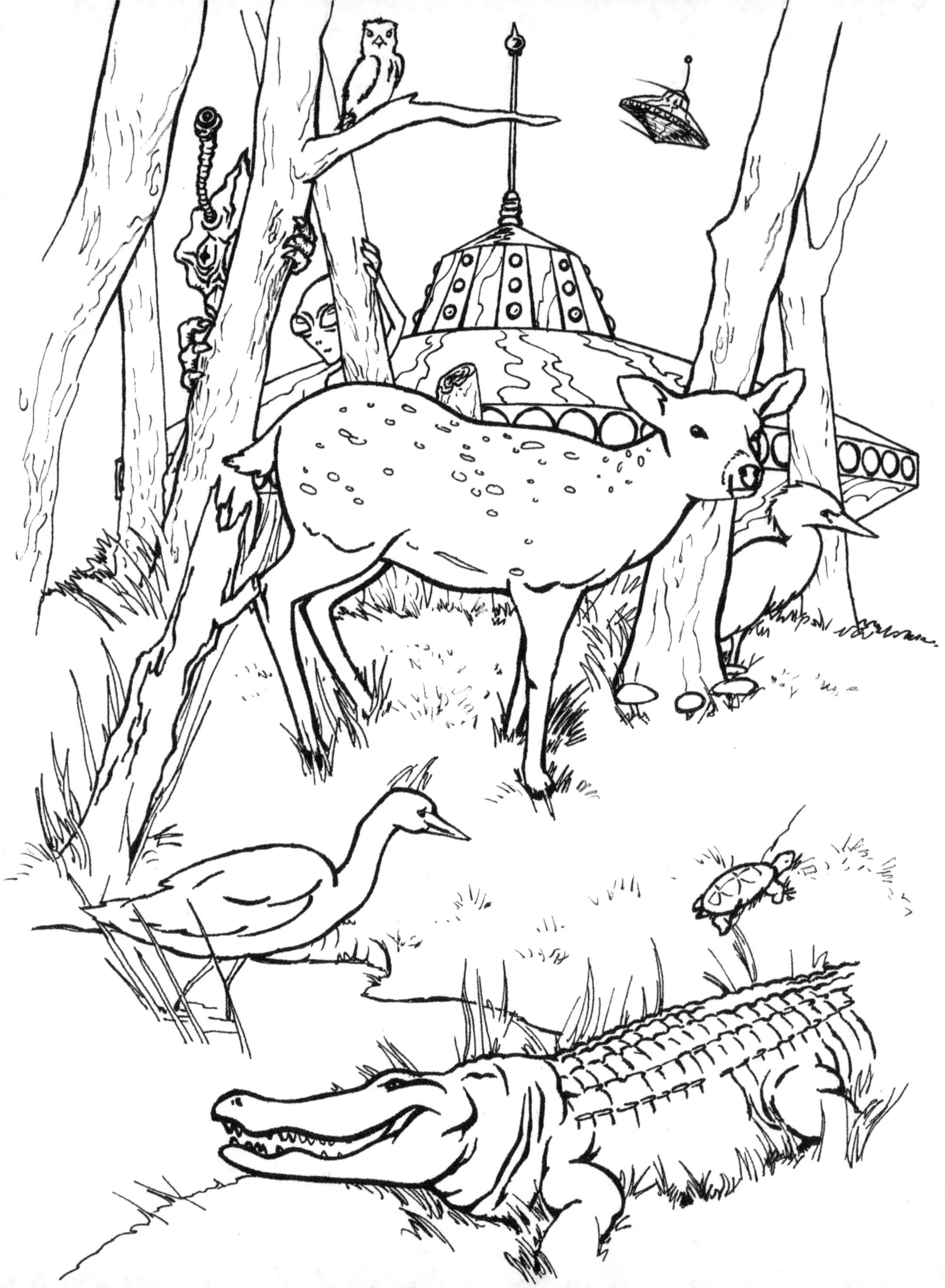

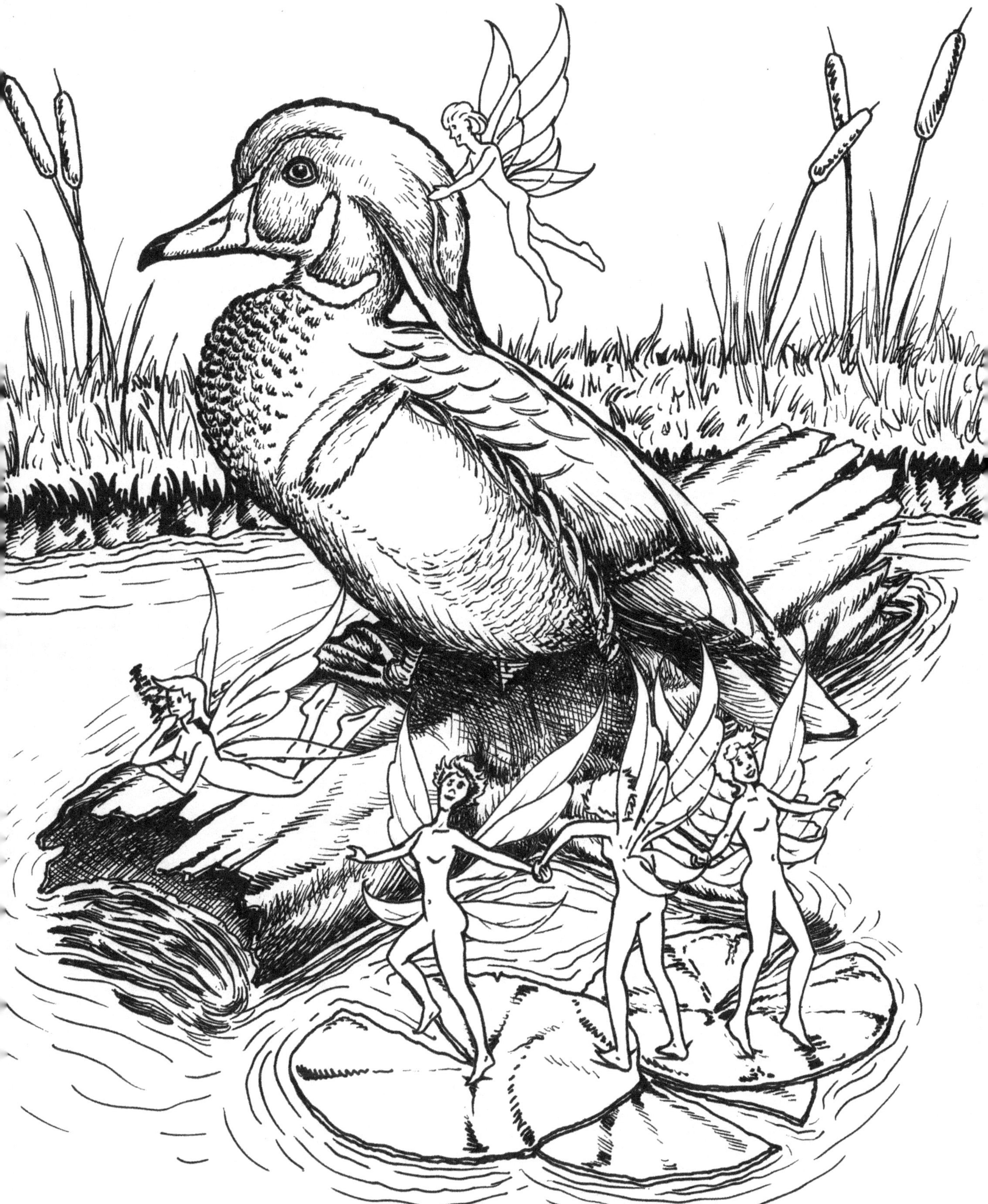

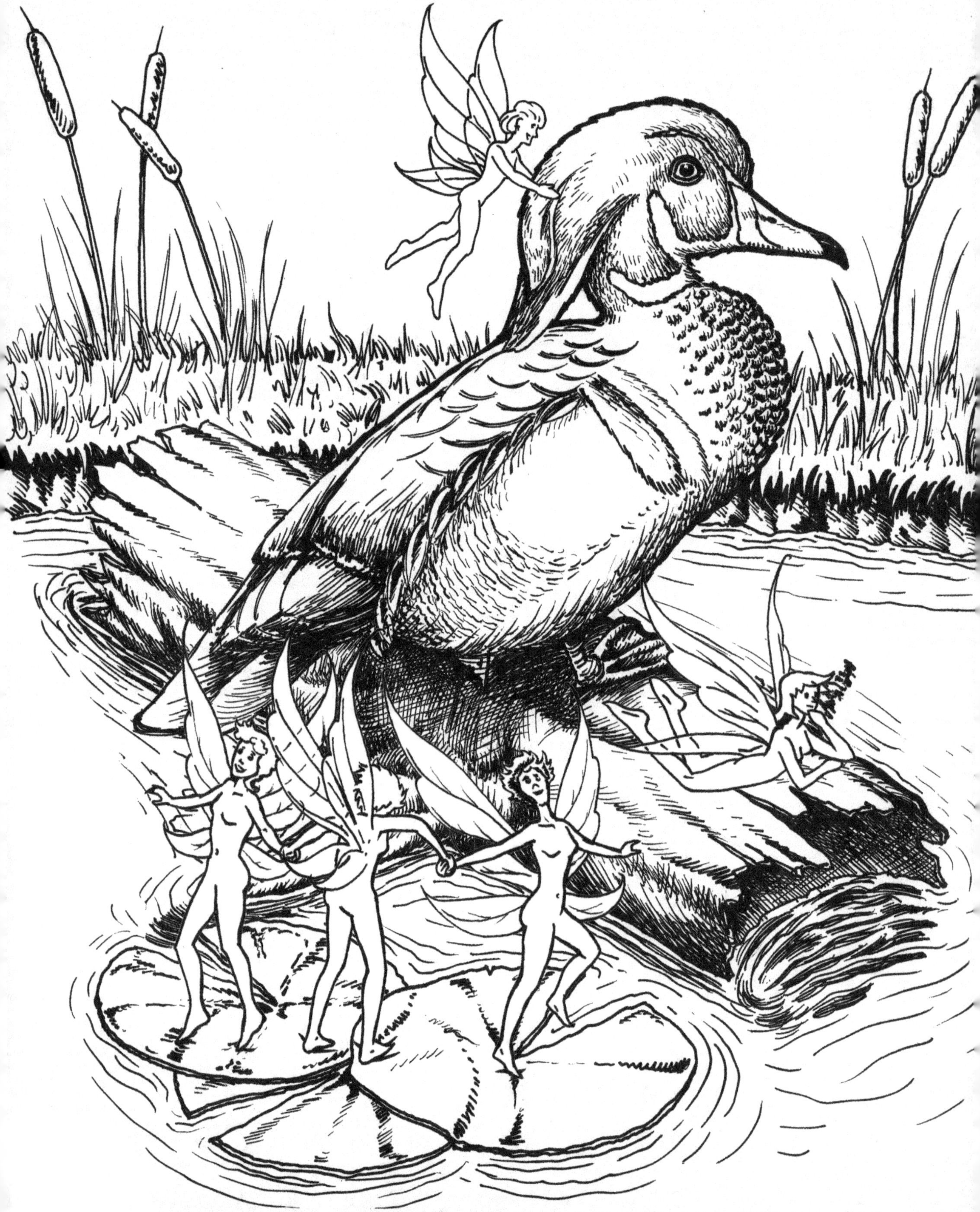

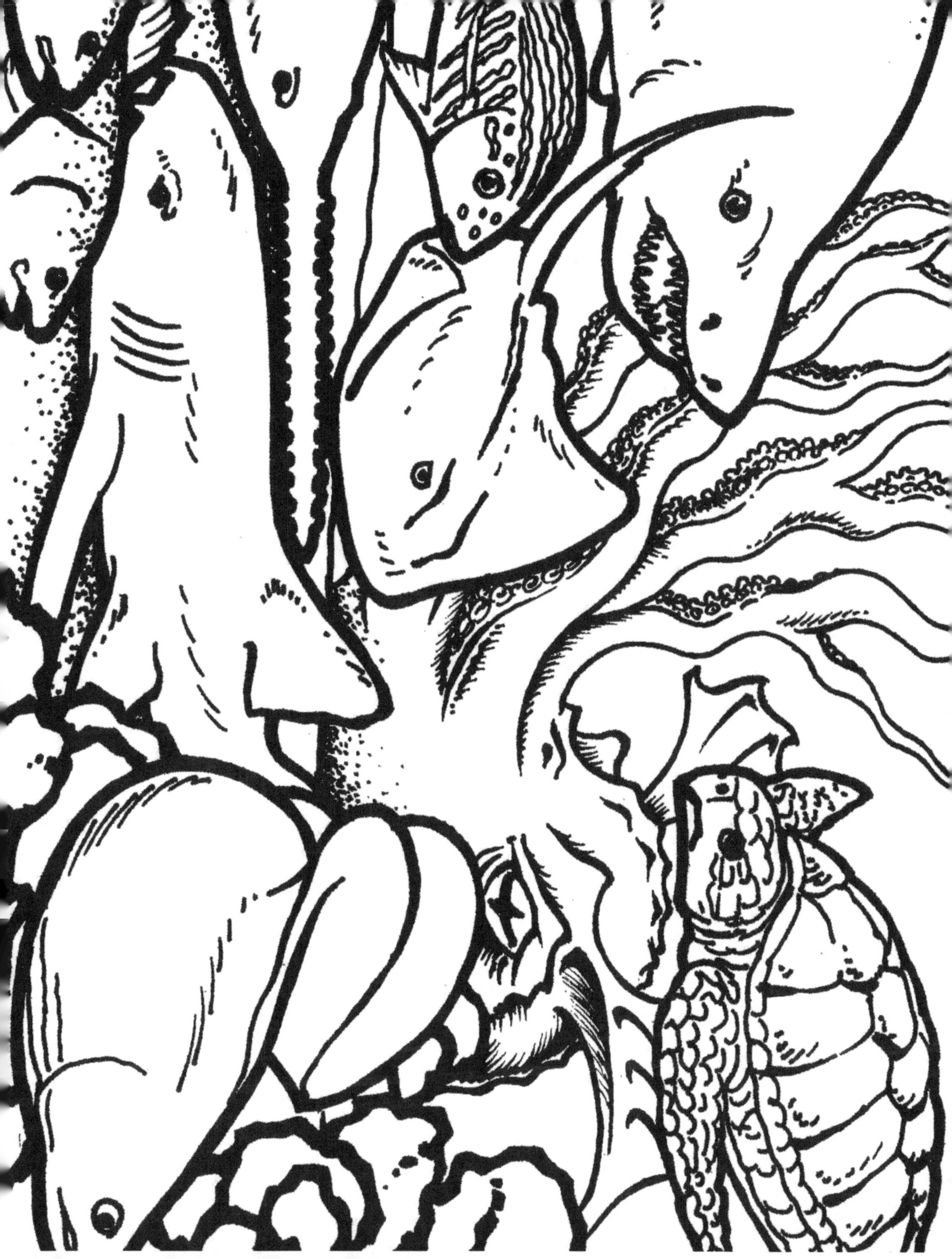

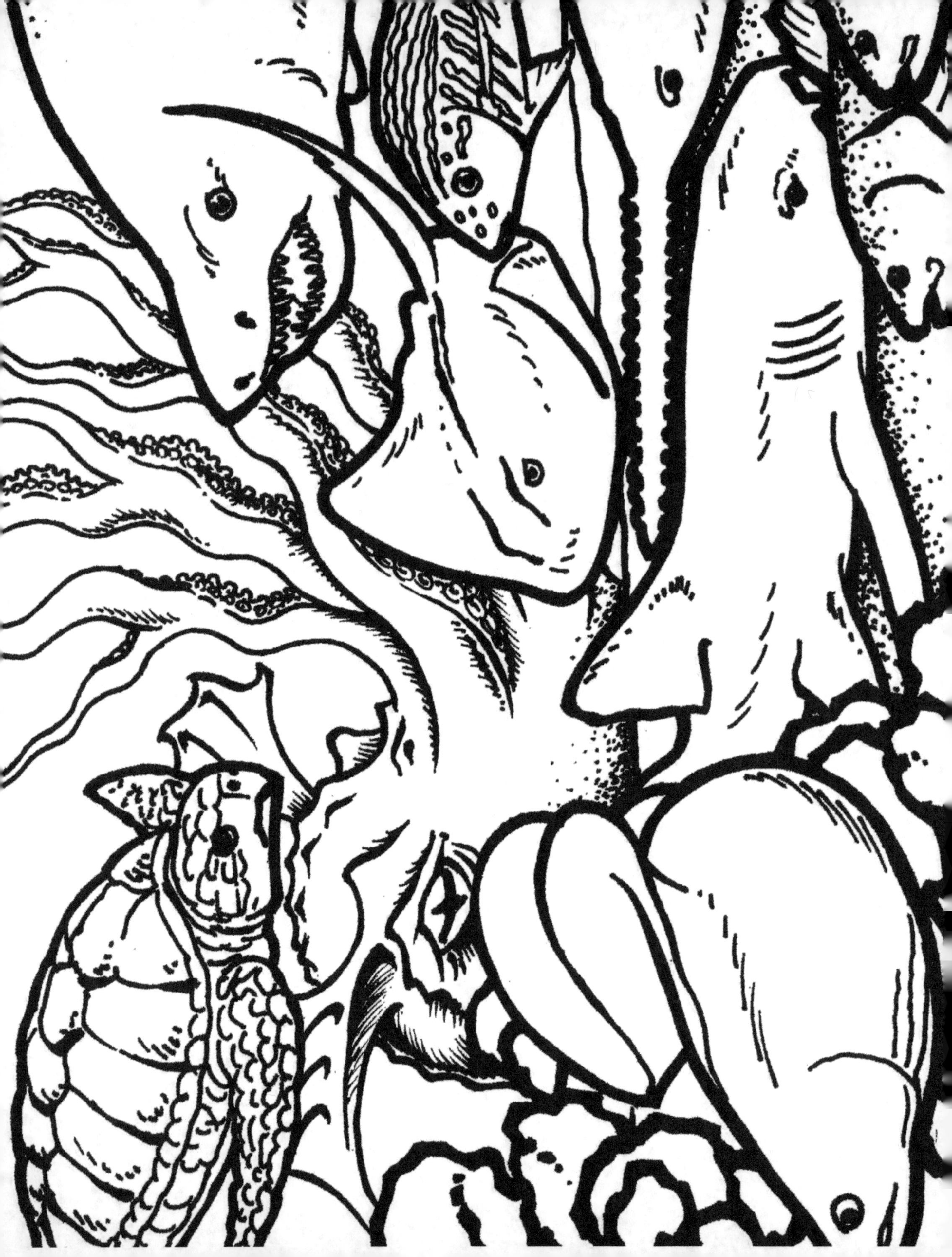

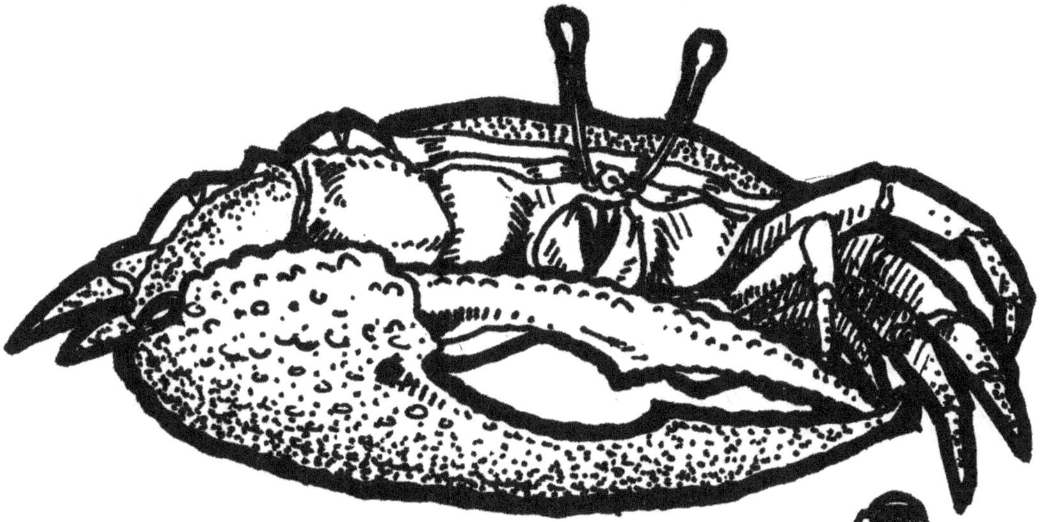
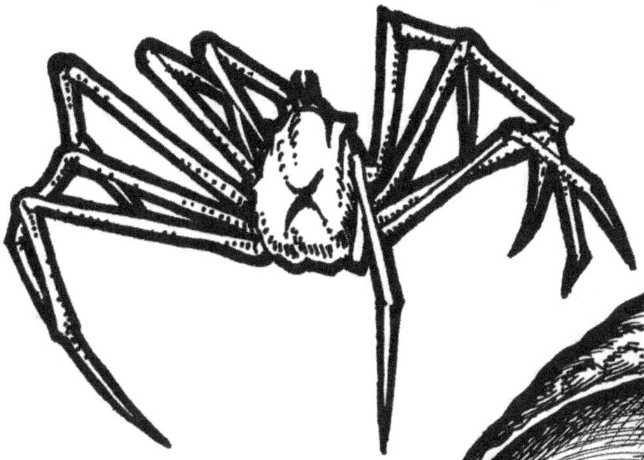
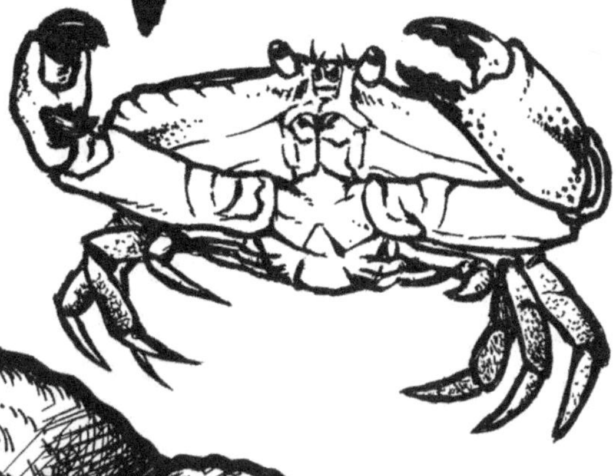
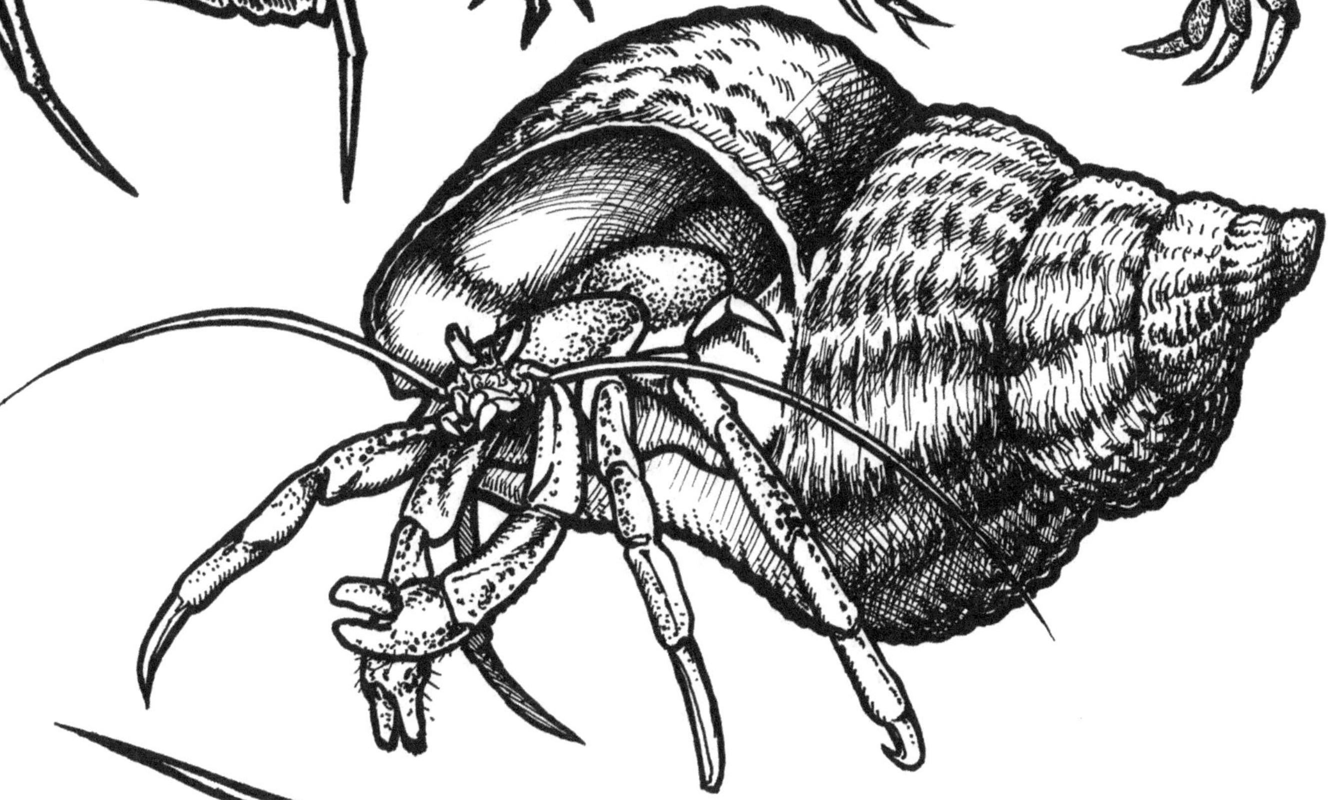

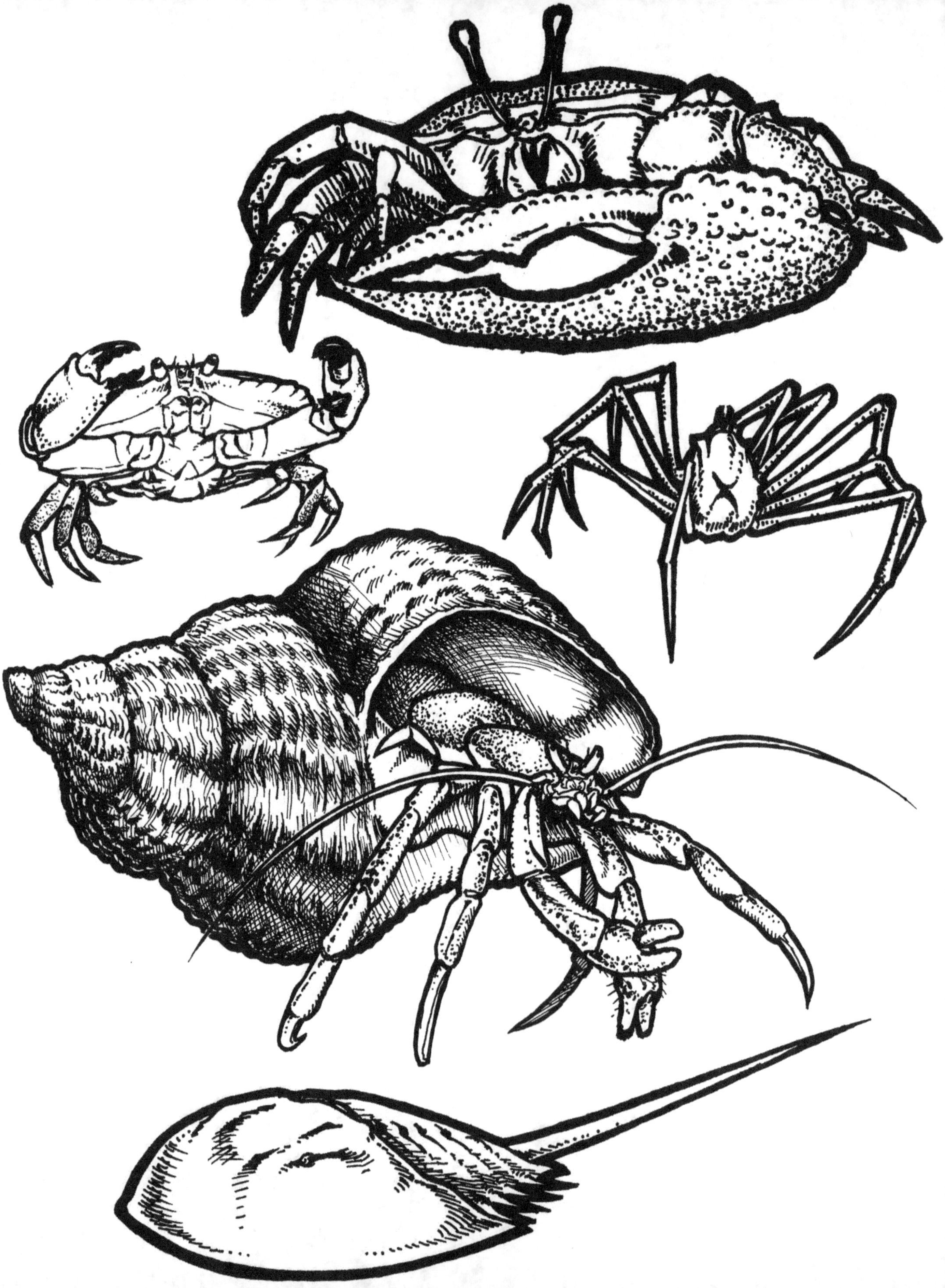

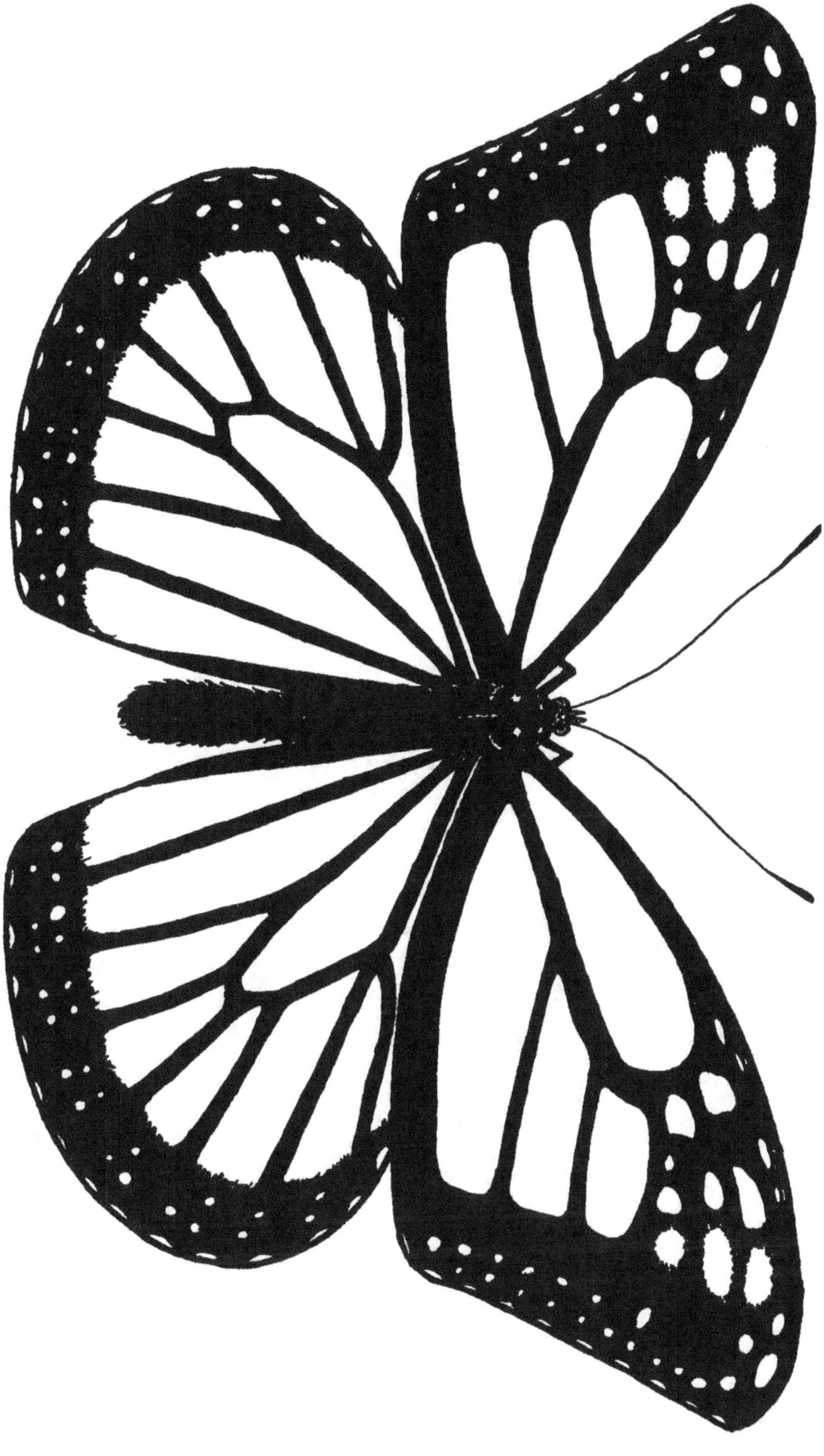

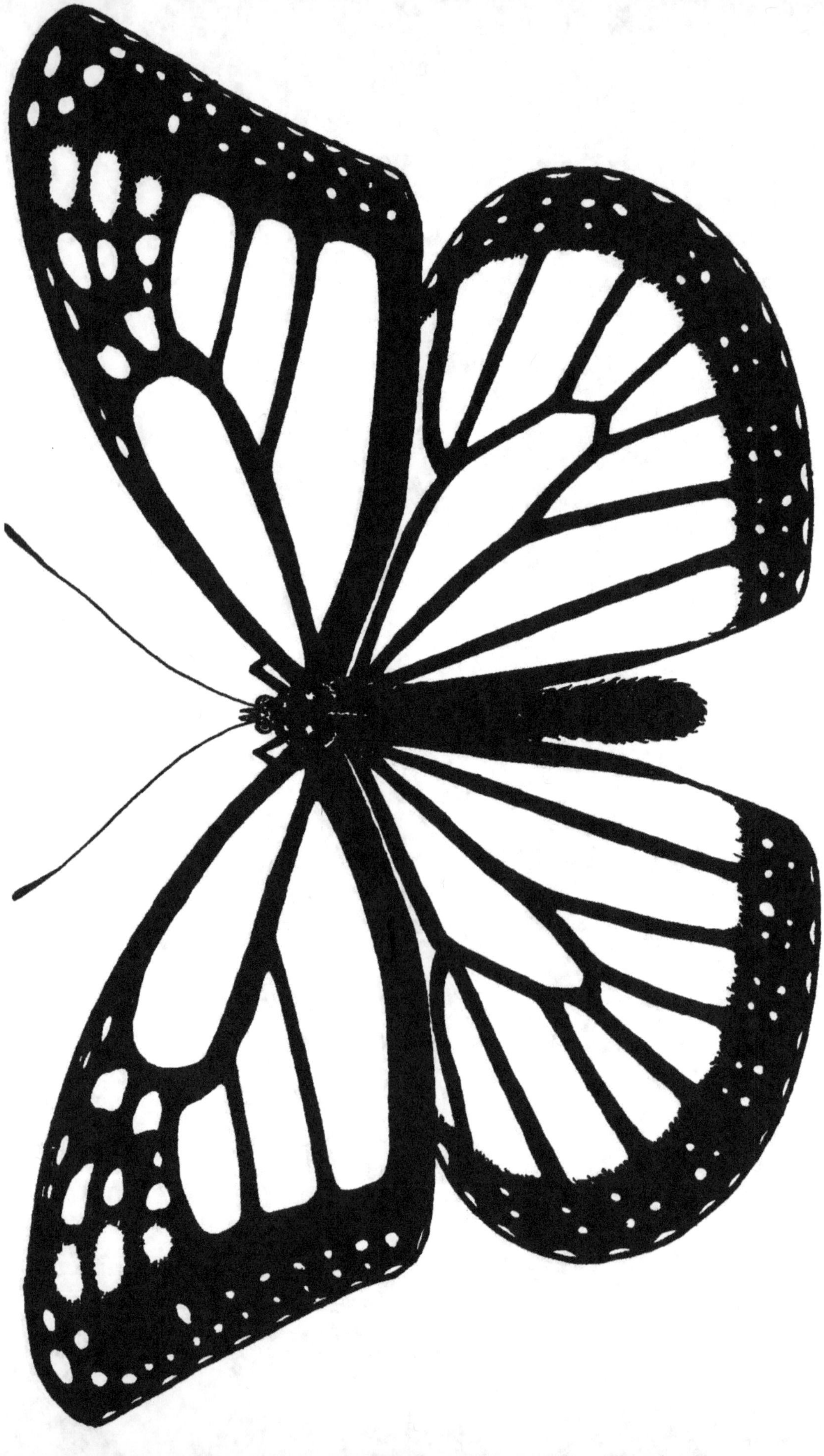

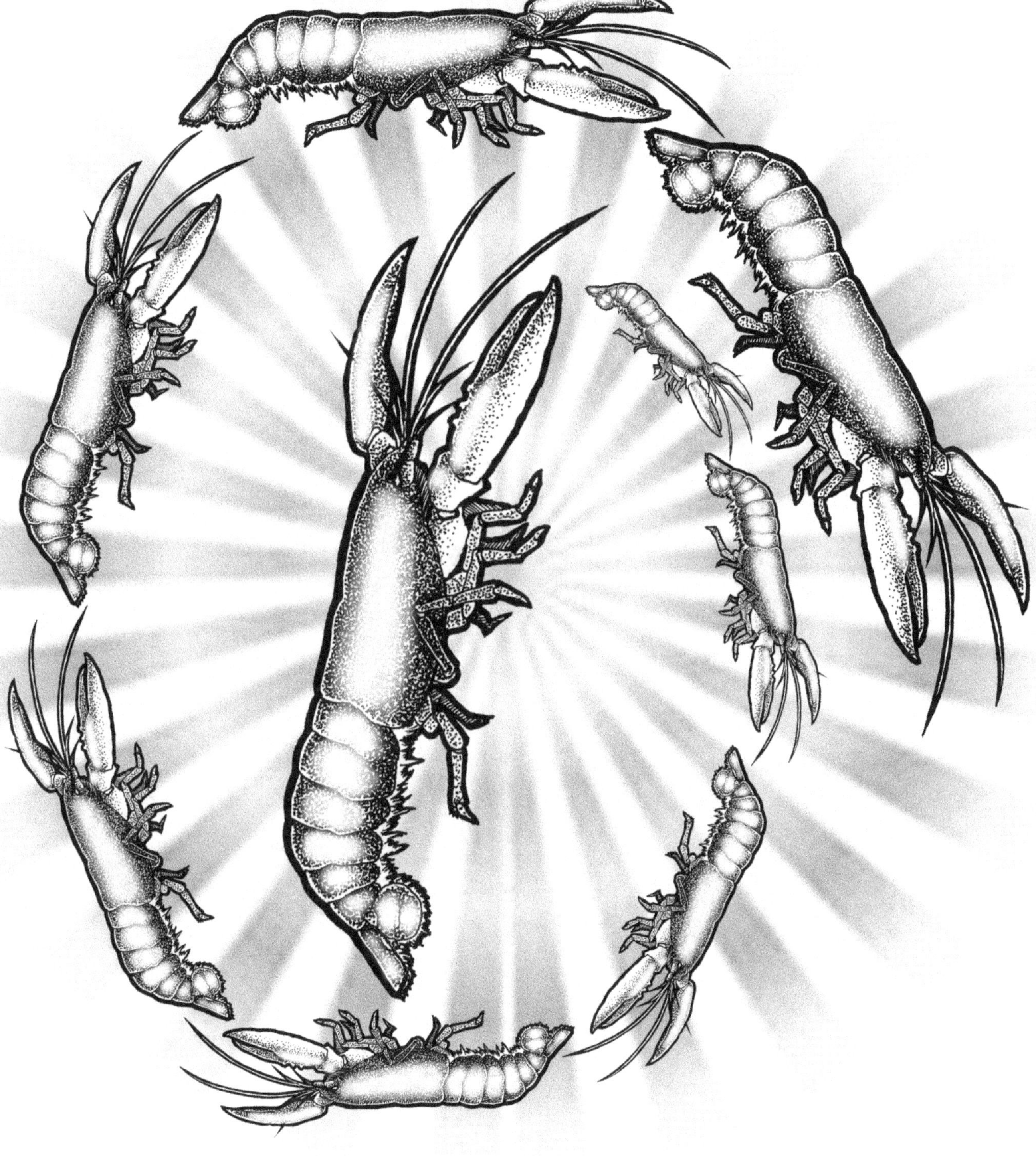

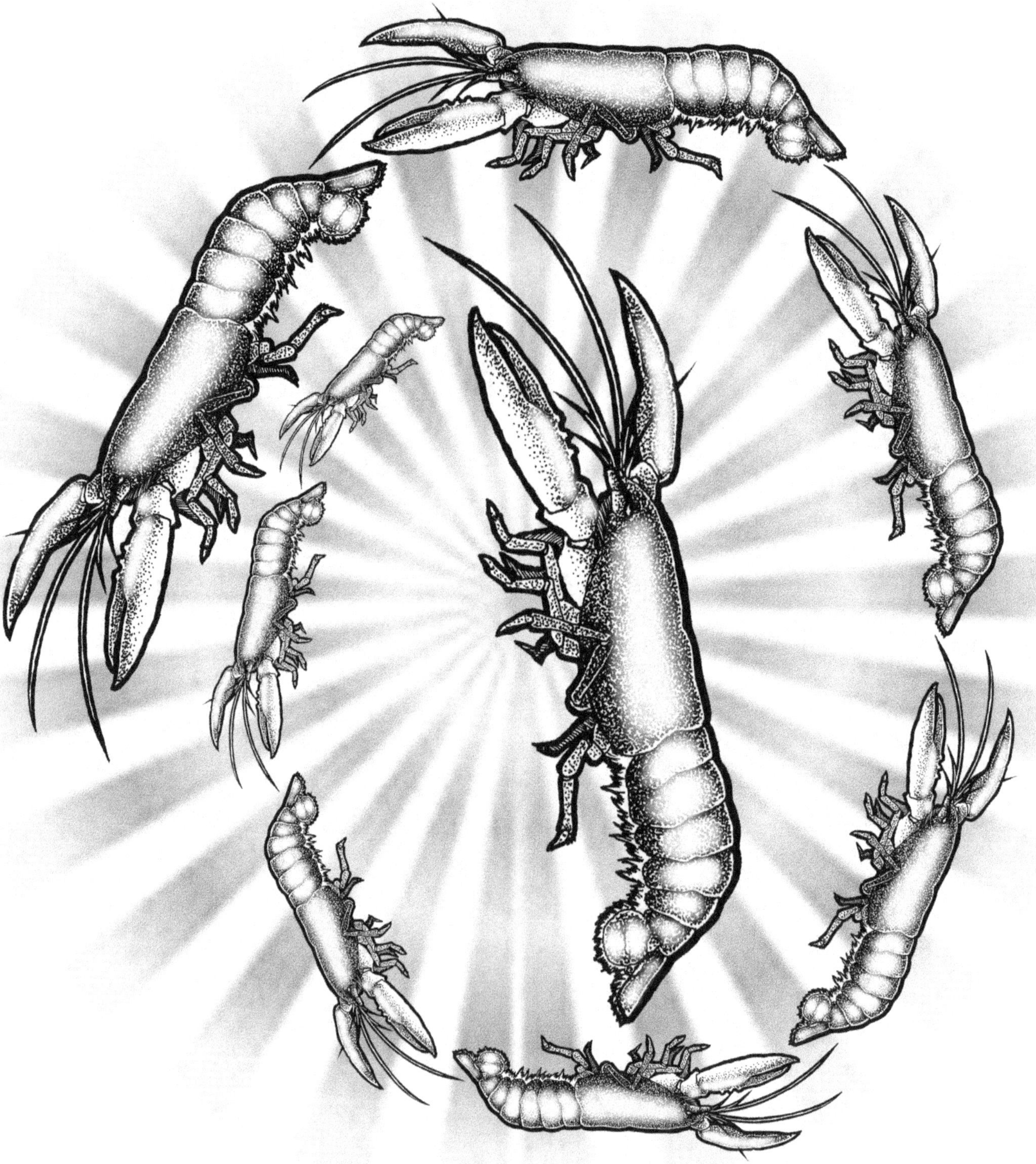

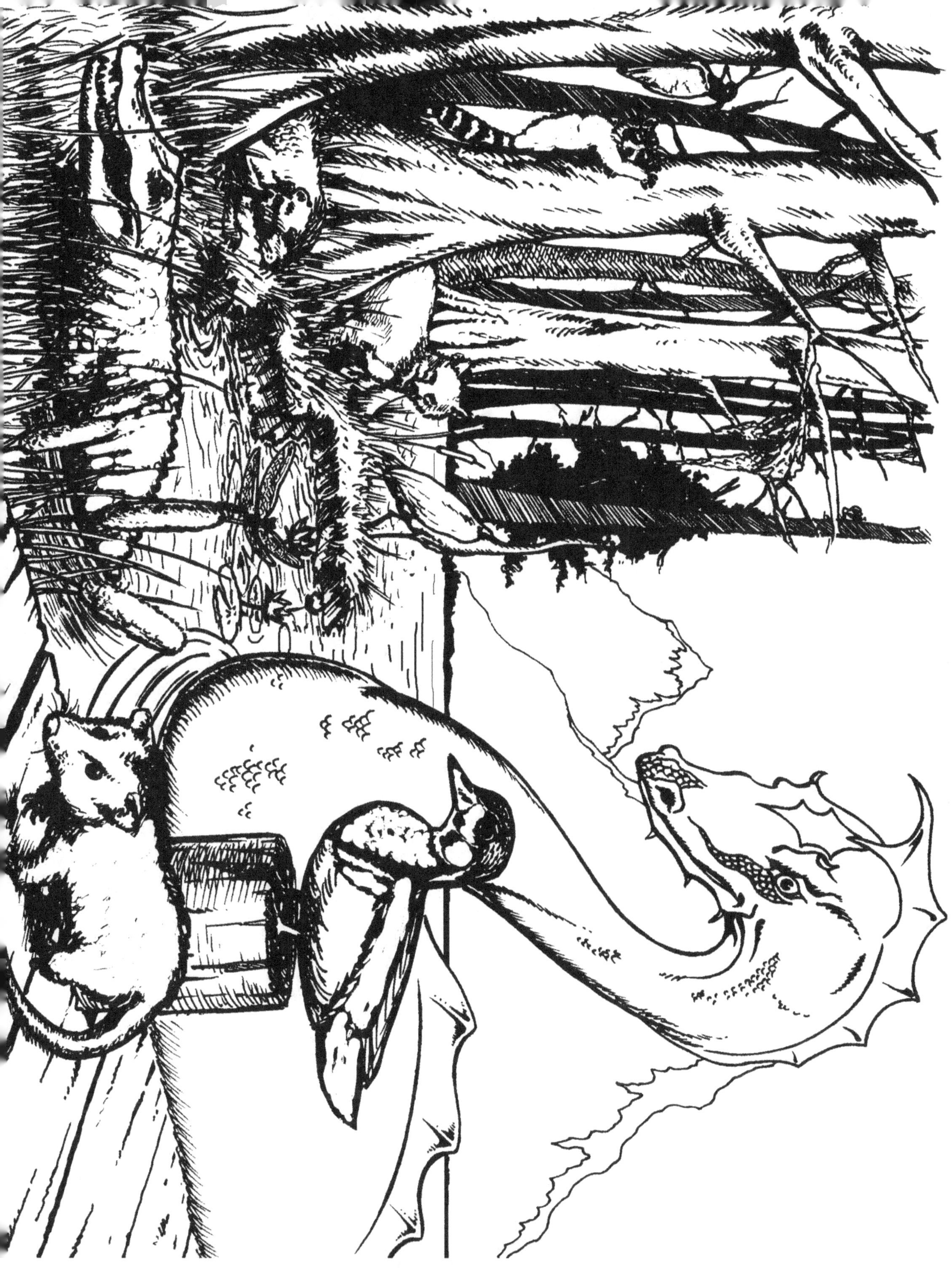

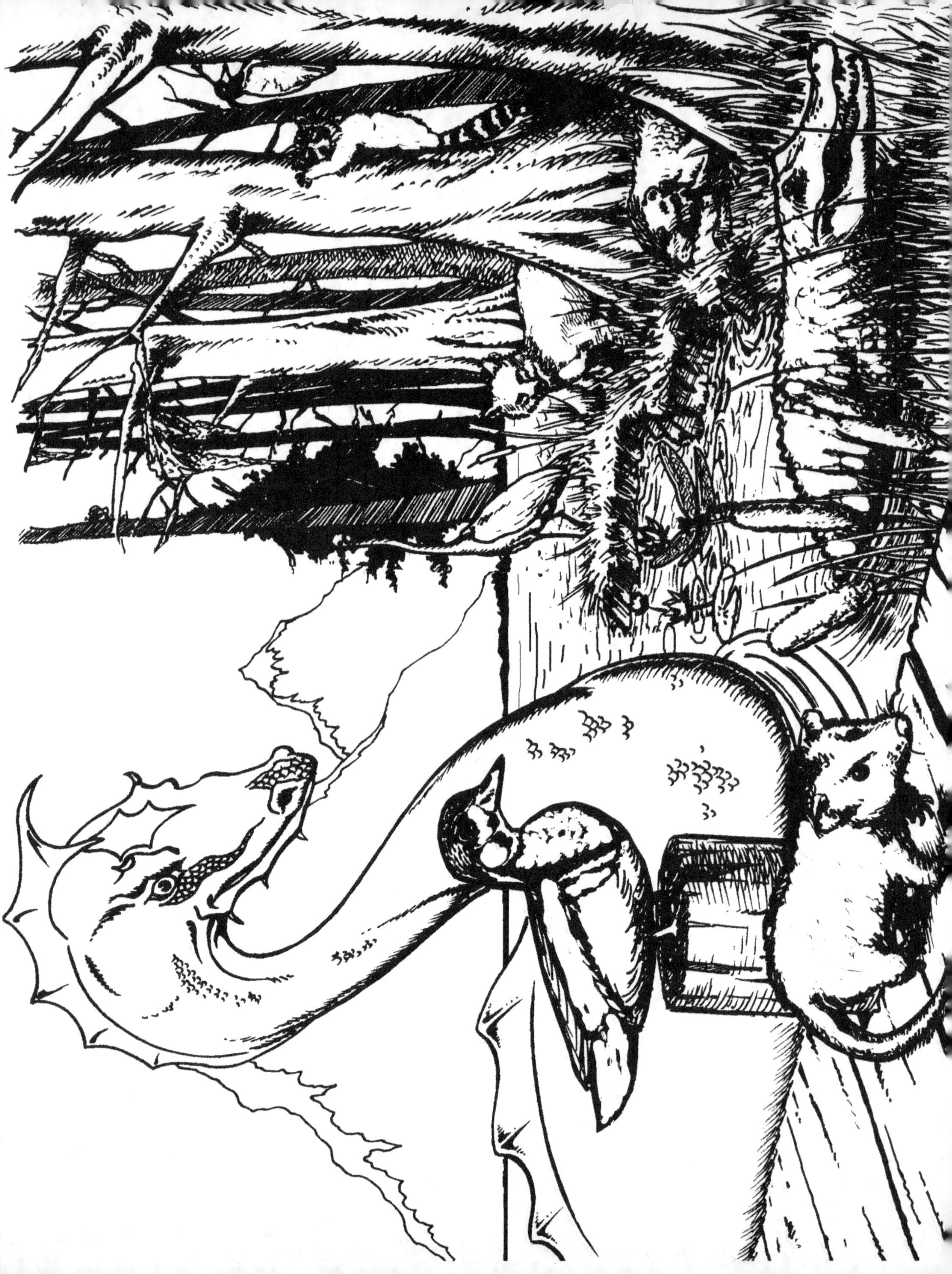

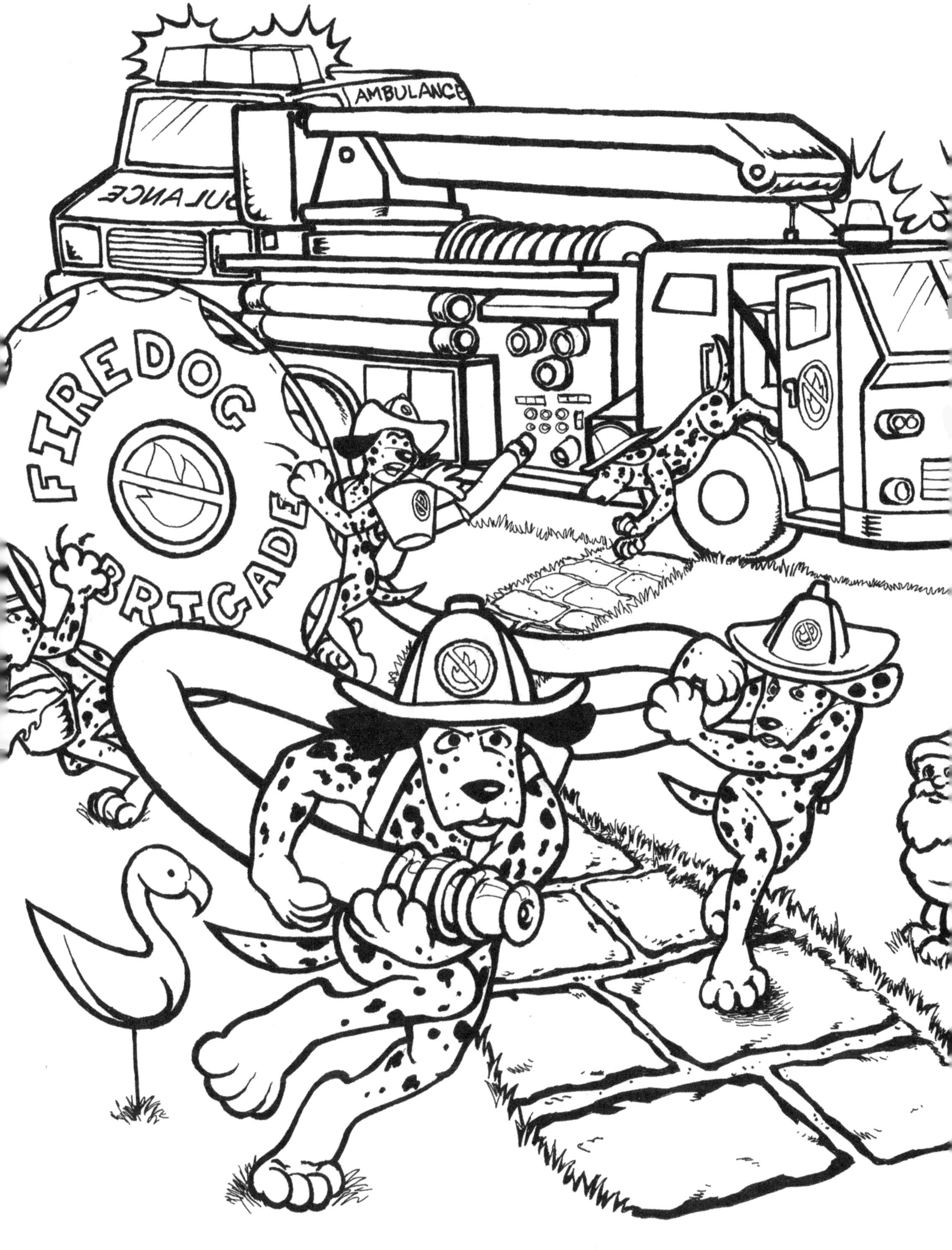
AMBULANCE
FIREDOG BRIGADE

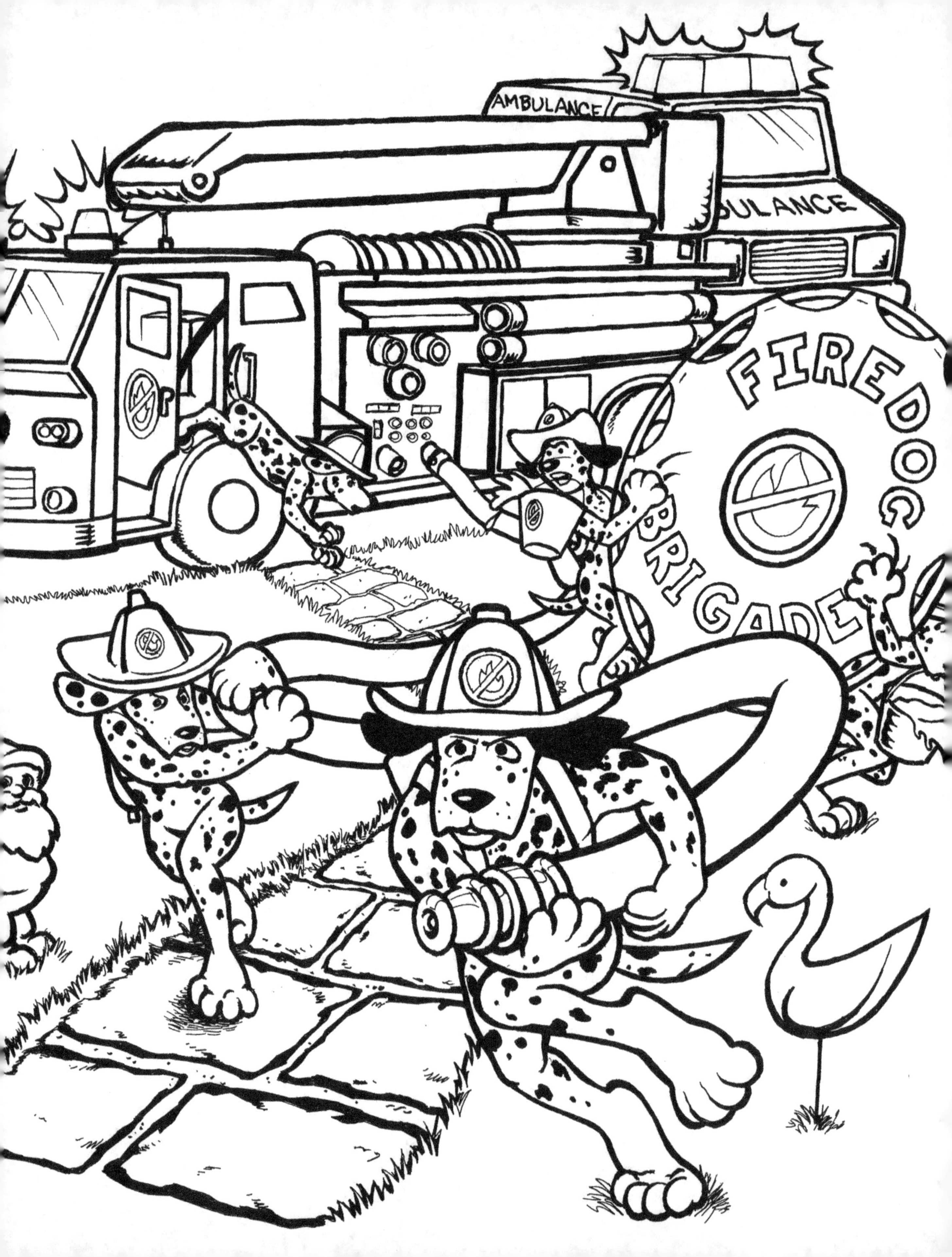
AMBULANCE
BULANCE
FIREDOG
BRIGADE

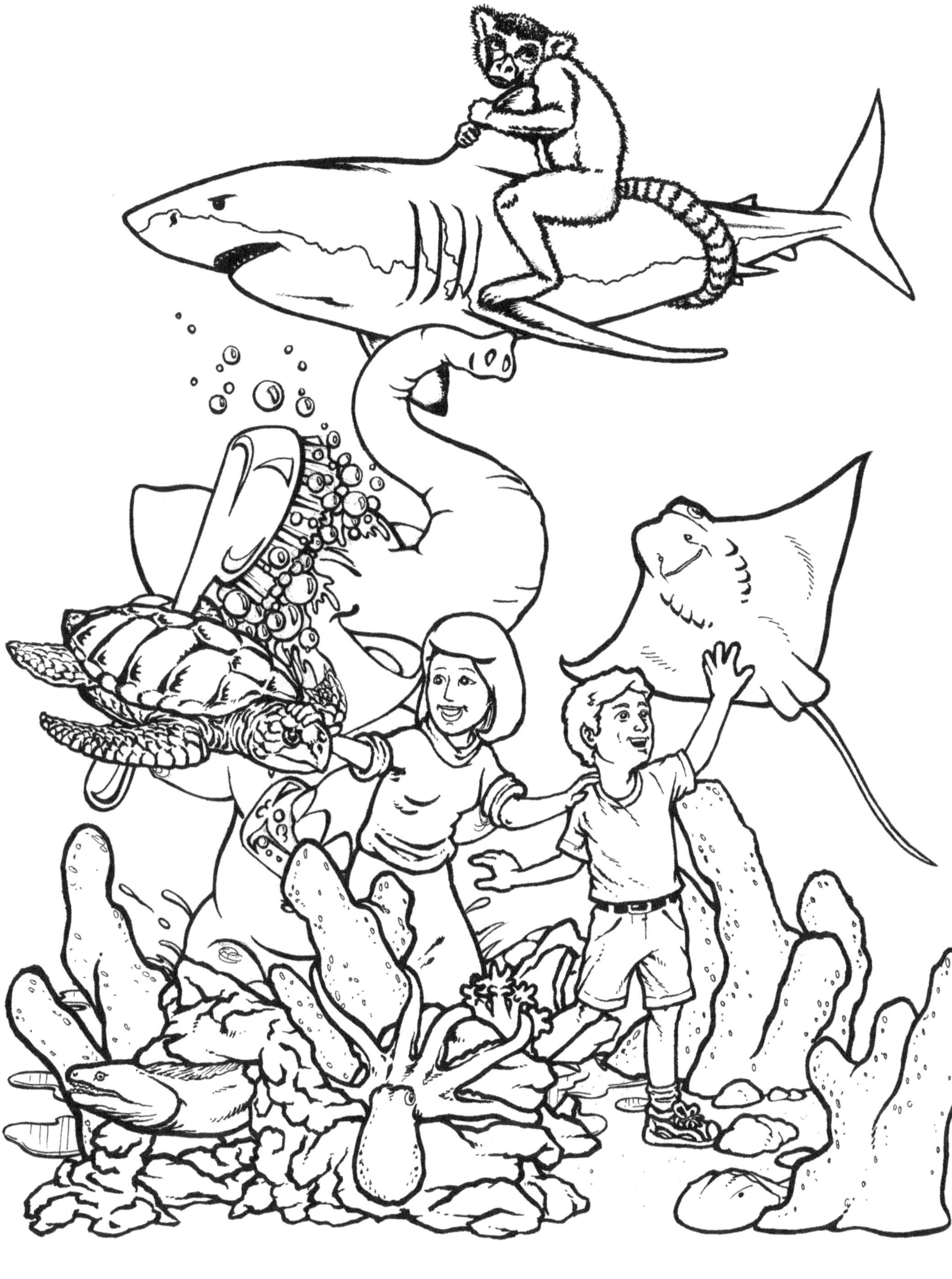

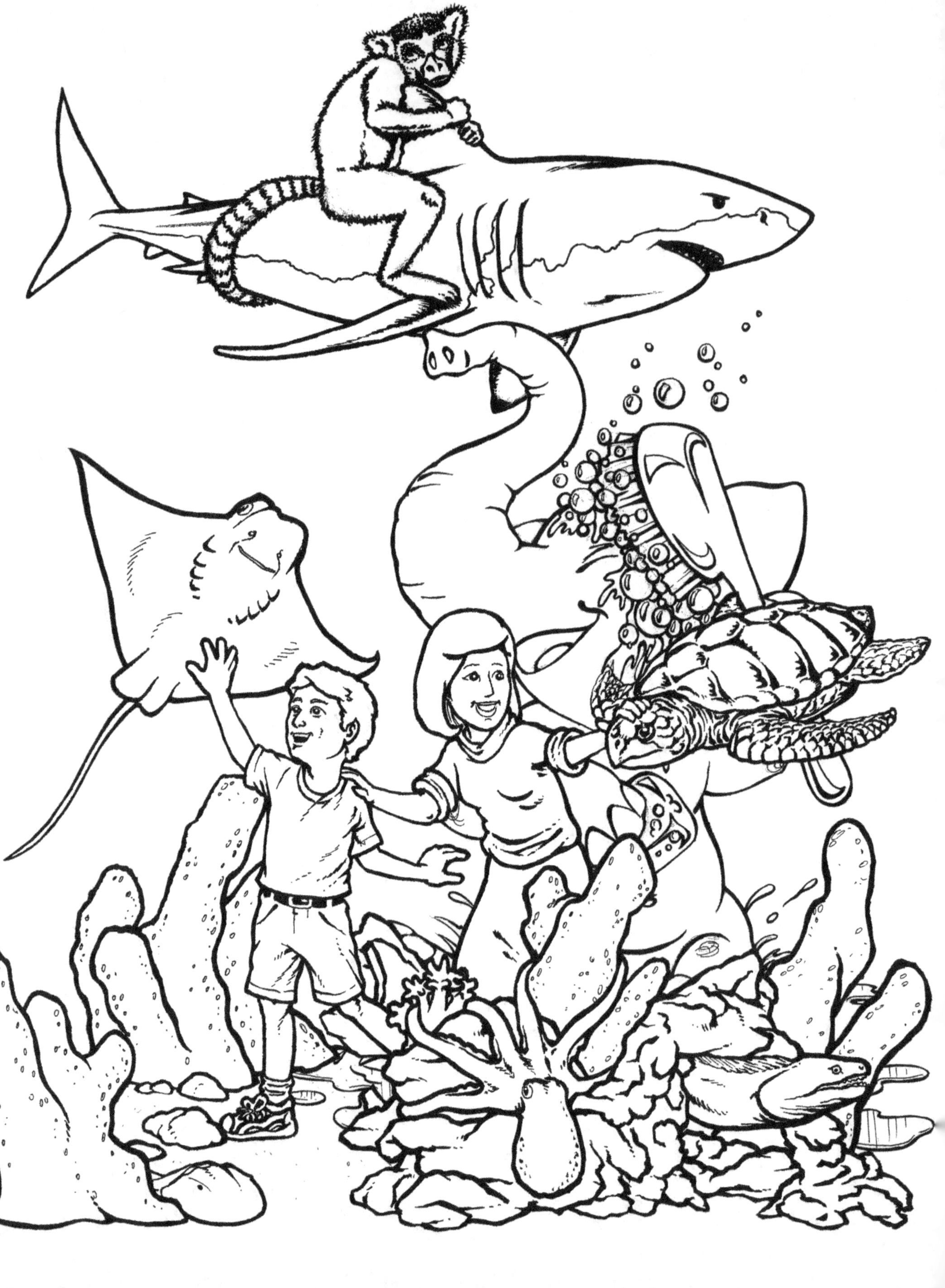

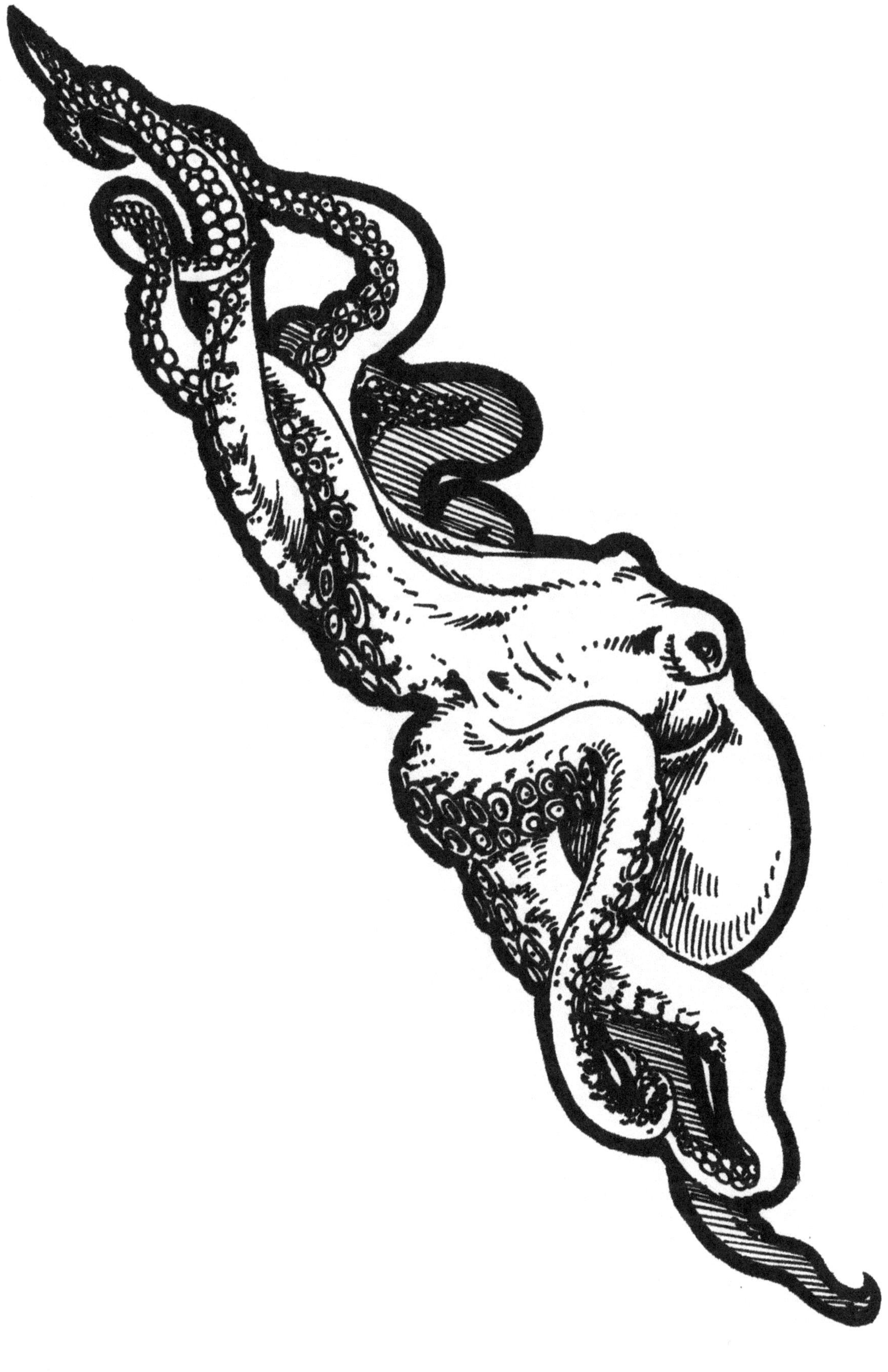

www.ingramcontent.com/pod-product-compliance
Lightning Source LLC
Chambersburg PA
CBHW080139240526
45468CB00009BA/2631
* 9 7 8 1 9 8 3 9 3 4 5 8 2 *